Big Cats in Tiny Dresser Drawers

By
Michael E. Ford

The cover is designed by the author

First Edition

Library of Congress Cataloging-in-Publication Data has been applied for

ISBN 978-1-257-80113-8

Hello!   Hello!

For anyone,
especially myself.

But you can give a try too if you want :)

This book was written in my apartment as a solution to throw my bullhorn into history as a dreamer. Most of my inspiration to continue with the project came from around the trolly tracks in East Village in downtown San Diego between 2009-2010. Not to mention; my jobs, art, women, travels, cuisine, memories and imagination played a part as well. There is no stable order in a chronological sense. It's page-for-page.

DONNIE ONCE SAID

"There is a little bug that hides in between the cracks in the sidewalks. If you don't walk around the fucking shit you can grab a bite. Scoop your eyes down in there and observe the landscape, as with anything. Tonight is not the night to be fucking around. If you think you're thinking to much you'll undoubtedly get sidetracked, but if you know how to use small utensils and your fingers aren't sweating heaps, everything should work out. Let them come to you - play hard to get. They'll be calling your name. As for me, well, I'm off to another barn for more work. I must say, this country life isn't what I thought it was going to be." –Donnie Reckless

Enough said, lets move on.

AWAY WITH THE BURNERR

I had been walking down a silent path toward patience. A self guided tour through a heavily wooded forest full of bad thoughts and recycled ideas. I needed something more. I went out one day and made it all happen. The restoration of peace was being built right before my eyes. A Spanish inspired colonel just steps form my favorite tea shoppe. This structure had been glistening in the sun for ages. What a treat!

The village almost seems back to normal again. There are not yet pies cooling on the windowsills of their horny cheating housewives. But the grass is green and it's always sunny. Yes, quite quaint indeed for a *young sir*. If you're in the moment then that's only the first step. You must be prepared to take full advantage of your position. Legs straight, arms by your side - and don't speak unless spoken to.

If people laugh before they cry then they are fucking morons. They're having too much fucking fun - even you know that. You have to cry over whatever. I cried over burnt toast in a crowded restaurant. Once they real-

2

ized they fucked up, they brought out a fresh order. It was not until then I laughed. It was not until then I ate the toast I had been longing for. I was happy.

What I've been listening to over the past few months does not constitute any logical system. This is the part where you're starting to realize that your interest for this structure is far more than a thread of innocent guesses. It is an obsession with numbers. There may be several different implications in the message. But you can rest assured that behind it, it's all numbers (and figures). They're *building* an empire. They were building a sand castle. We were building desserts from a bathtub full of ice cream and assorted toppings.

MAX △
ERMA
BOBBY
GOATS

ARE YOU A MOTHER FUCKING CRACKHEAD?

I'm guessing that you probably are. I honestly cannot believe how much you disgust me. The whole thing is impossible. For me, trying to be nice to you is harder than trying to piss out of my mouth. I must be hallucinating, the way you continue to speak to me. You are a hound muffin running on high I tell you. That's just what I said too.

Are you constantly surrounded by red brick walls and dead grass? Do you reside on the Eastern side of any metropolitan area? Do you live in a brownish-carpeted apartment without a washer/dryer? If you answered yes to one of theses questions, you may be well on your way to becoming a full-blown bottom feeder.

He is scratching his neck and asking about the steak. He is scratching his neck and asking about the steak. He is scratching his neck and asking about the steak. He is scratching his neck and asking about the steak. He wants to know how it is prepared and what local farm the meat came from. He

4

wants some information about the steak he
will eat.

I made a sandwich that was bound by
alpha sprouts and sprayed with garlic oil. It
was one hell of a controversy in my house-
hold. It always made a *huge mess* and it stunk
up the place like a hawt wedge of parm would.
But it was healthy. Sometimes you have to
look past the scent and bite into the thickness
of it all. Scrub some dirt off the bun if need
be.

WISH LIST, COOL IT BABY

I want to dissect the part of the body where emotion triggers motion. I want to eat those neurotransmitters with a house dressing. All this action potential is keeping me shivering on the edge of my seat. The sun shines through the window so bright it almost *burns* a hole in the floor. I can see dust particles flying around like traffic in a busy city. At the time I was thinking it was my dandruff activating.

Senior prom? *Hmmmm*, didn't go. Next question please.

The last time I saw a caterpillar I threw it in somebody's burger when they weren't looking. Is that fucked up? Didn't think so. I also put a live ant in someone's cigarette before. Emptied out half the tobacco, shoved the little guy in there and filled it back up with the *back-ho*. It popped when the cherry got to it. Clueless. Like the shoe company, or was it a movie?

I've lit shit in a paper bag on fire before. I had to. The most challenging part I think was trying to poop into the bag. Or are you just supposed to use dog poop? No way, human poop is better. It shows dedication. *Plus*, it melts faster.

Let me tell you about when I use to unroll rolls of toilet paper, get them dripping wet, ball them up like softballs, and nail shitty cars with them. Or better yet, get it soaking wet with rubbing alcohol and light it on fire. It explodes like your uncles gull bladder. *Brown buckets of paint for free.*

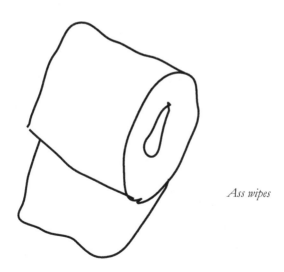

Ass wipes

THE CHAMPAGNE ROOM!

Well what a crock of shit that whole entire thing was. Lions and hula-hoops? *Ummm*, not impressed. I was more impressed when I found out there was more to life then WWF and Doritos.

SALLY, SCRAM

Sally walks without her baggage
Sally walks without her precautions
Sally forgot her cell phone in the cab
Sally took off her panties for another guy
Sally doesn't know how to shop for food
Sally has deep dark secrets
Sally smokes cigarettes
Sally drinks lots of booze
Sally tells her parent's she's doing "ok" when they ask
Sally doesn't return your phone calls
*Sally thinks she's the first person to listen to **60**'s rock*
Sally is the only person who shops at thrift stores
Sally likes a free ride
Sally cannot be tamed
Sally seems to be very unhealthy
Sally doesn't have a box to think outside of
Sally is only here because you brought her here
Sally doesn't respect anyone
Sally doesn't respect herself
Sally thinks she can continue to get what she wants
Sally will be rung out and dried
Sally will not be able to fight the current
Sally will be carried away by the birds

THE SENTIMENTALIST

It was not until **2008** that I had realized the *most popular* girl in school was, and always will be, Mona Lisa. Think about it.
Anyways, more to the point; A good reach is
all that matters. I'm not talking about reach-
arounds either. Over the shoulder, through
the leg? Fuck it. Suck it? Touch it?

I know this one girl who keeps a shit
load of chicken in the freezer. It's gross.
Gizzard lollipops.

SICKLE CELL RESEARCH

Science says hello to sickle cell research. They shake hands. Everyone here
knows they're here to do business. There is
no holding back now. They finish the food,
science signs the check. Sickle cell research
leans over and whispers "every scientist is Jesus now" into science's ear. Science starts
laughing and says "not that again."

ABOUT TERRY

One large pizza was far to much goodness for young Terry so he stopped eating. Put his old mug down and stopped all together. I take it, it had something to do with Terry's long hike tomorrow. Planning ahead was one of Terry's most prominent features, *scheduling features*.

Have you ever met a run on sentence before?

If you were lucky enough to catch Terry on a Sunday then you'd know that Terry's planner was booked up until at least Thursday and that he'd have to find time somewhere closer to Saturday to pencil you in for a little *happy-go-lucky* face time.

He had become more amused with hardening his gourd worrying about lesser issues, like leaking sinks and whether or not the deer were being starved. Because someone or something kept stealing the salt blocks off the red woods he had nailed them to.

He is now playing, he is really playing! Scratches on the neckk, HOLY SHIT! He's eating steak. **12** ounces of shit if you ask any other patron. "Not putting a ring on that steak if you catch my drift (wood)" said Terry. Terry says "if its math, it's science! And I can't stand 'em!".

One day Terry went to the store looking for Pop-Tarts. However, as soon as he sensed there'd be dust on the tops of those boxes he was quick to turn around and exit the store. He'd been trying to come up with an easy breakfast. Preferably something that would shadow a treat. Pop-Tarts was its game, Pop-Tarts was its name.

If Terry should ever see Keebler's cheese and peanut butter cracker sandwiches then you can bet he'll pick up a few boxes and stash most of them in his glove box. He prefers to eat them before or after stressful business meetings. But he notes that crackers certainly don't help stop the sweat factory on his forehead. Which seems to be over staffed.

"Standardized testing right down the hall sir. Rabbit door step was right next to it" said the lonely nurse. She is not really here, just always giving direction. Terry can handle it though, his heart is **35**psi.

HOUSEHOLD BOUNDRIES

Yesterday my friend told me he was clearing out his closet. I paused for a second and then asked, "Are you planning on keeping anything this time around?" He promptly responded, "Not planning on it." I knew he would end up saving something. I just knew it. Surely his tadpole swimmers badge would be revived. I'm also guessing he'll save his pogs.

My friend has one of those Talkboy's, you know that voice recorder Macaulay Culkin uses in *Home Alone 2*? Yeah, he's got that. I've had my eyes on it for quite some time. The weird thing about it is, is that I have no idea why. I have absolutely no desire to own his Talkboy, or any voice recorder (not true). I just keep my eyes on it. I keep staring at it like a magic jeannie is going to *fart* out and give me a wish, or a popsicle, or Yankees tickets.

POOF!

It got me thinking! I took the wheel toward Old Man's Cave. They say I have the blood, but do I have the scent? I spent so much time being held down, I forgot what it was like to stand up. Just kidding, I've never sat down in my life. I'm more on edge than Donnie Reckless. He's been battered and fried against my hard times for flavor. Texture.

The ingredients that we use are native to the land, and native to our spirits. The red clay represents the liver and the dark blues represent our hearts. To the beginning we shall return. We are more monster than we think. We are civil being evil.

MOOSE MAN

Moose Man, Moose Man
The man with the thoughts
Every good deed gets market with red dots
On with the wind which every man floats
On down the path where every man floats
Good deeds, good deeds, where every man knows
At last! Good deeds, now everyone knows!
But young Moose Man, young Moose Man
Who sits, who waits alone
The crying agony that stains his throne
Overthrown and overgrown by the youths of his tribe
His heavy following has subsided
His campsite has grown fury
The blue on the trees is not welcoming anymore
Old Moose Man, old Moose Man
Where do you reside?

"Moose Man was last spotted on December
17th **1988**. A collection of his footprints can
be found on display at the Mahogany St. Ar-
thur's Museum of Moose Men located firmly
on the tip of Edmonton, Canada"
  –Resources

VANTAGE POINT

Its not going to happen for you every-day, but on occasion, you will be standing knee deep in vantage point. What a hounding toll it will take. Much complacency is sure to follow. One skill you will capture is how to use your instinct. Quickness is in the eyes. *Tri-noculars* are in tune for this mission. Will you be ready to pack up and scout when the doorbell rings?

I'm ringing like a bell. My time spent here does not amount to any sort of "trade in". I also had to leave a few items un-checked due to time allowances and permission rights. Yes, it's a strange, strange duty to uphold. My personal imagery is counter-weight against what is expected of it. I intend to keep calm in this moment of epiphany. I will ransack the dressers and try on different clothing. Pinches of nutmeg my darling.

Trade in.

FINE GRANULARITY

Open your mouth. Here come the sprinkles of substance, imagine you're a gold fish. You're in a bowl that holds less than **1.5** gallons of water, and you're by your lonesome. You are any **9** year old's dream come true for only **4** days. Your self-pride cannot compete with the attention span of a **9** year old. So you're stuck in a bowl, just waiting for the grains to descend again. It's your only moment of satisfaction. The sound of the toilet flushing from the next room sounds like Beethoven.

A note

BANKING ON THE NOTABLE

One time I had a delayed flight from Chicago to Reno. I decided to stick myself in a bar for a few hours. I had a butterfly bow-tie on. I could tell the bartender was searching for common ground. Out of spite I asked him, "How do you like working here at O'Hare?" He firmly responded, "I'd rather be dead." At this point I knew things were about to get interesting. I quickly looked both directions and asked, "O ya? What would you be doing with yourself then?" The bartender took a crumpled up magazine page out of his pocket. You could tell it was from a magazine, from the gloss. It was a photo of a reindeer from a National Geographic. "Do you believe in reincarnation?" I asked. He whispered a prolonged "yes". It was creeper status. It was now my turn to *firmly* reply, "If you believe in reincarnation then how do you explain overpopulation?" I asked. He didn't know what to say, he stood there for about 8 seconds and said, "I just wanna work for Santa." We didn't speak after that and he gave me all my drinks for free.

DISPOSALABLE MODESTY

You're always drinking it up. You keep pointing out everything you don't see fit. You start knocking things down and making things fit. I can feel the ground shaking and I know you've made contact. You've changed the world around me, now its blood and combat.

You can fly around like a bird all day but you're only as brave as the poop that spews from your butt hole.

So keep it up.

Keep it up, mother fucker!

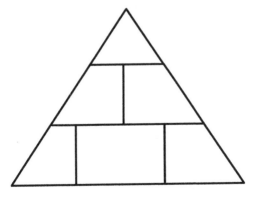

SWINGING LOW

I know this kid named Tony, and no, he's not Italian. He's a fucking idiot. I met him at camp when I was **12**. Just kidding, I was nearly **11**. There was a swimming pool that all the campers were forced to swim in for one hour out of the day. It was an "activity". I am still convinced it was just a front for the camp counselors to sneak off and pop the zits off of each others ass' while they fucked intensely. Anyways, whenever we got tucked in at the pool Tony would always hang out in the shallow end. He would go to the edge of the pool, find a jet, and survey the landscape. He would barely lean out of the pool, holding himself up by his elbows. He would secretly have his cock pressed up against the air jet until he came. His eyes would roll back and his hair would stand straight up. By the time he was finished it looked like he got electrocuted. I mean, he was pretty much electrocuting his frenulum with air. Sorry Tony.

TRASH REPORT

Are you lying there awake? Or are you taking another shit in the bucket? Your contribution is greatly admired by those constipated. The darkness of it all, I hope they turn a black light on at some point. Whatever grows in the night seems to be growing upward. My wife is changing out her tampon in the bathroom. *Better not be making a mess again either.* She wants me to fuck her ass. She got so horny. I noticed there were wet spots on the bedding from before she got up. She crawled back into bed. Ten minutes later she was left with a cream pie. More wet spots on the bedding too.

MISSION GORGE

I'm astounded by what these children think they can get away with. Chicken crack corn. I mean, these kids are just lobbyists. They're not parliaments, they don't speak on other peoples behalves. They're not bacon, they don't make everything better. They're going nowhere but at least they're standing their ground. I have to admit, I'm kind of *jelly* of it all. Pre-gem, post-gorge...post-kong, modern world. A perfect example of an advanced grade. A movement stronger than whiplash. A movement bigger than you or I.

I started teaching enlightenment classes at this cultural center. It's mostly just weirdo's that show up. There is a yoga class after my seminar so I get a lot of those guys, stretching in the background and what not. I thought I could reach out to these kids but all they care about is electricity. I think I'm going back on the market at the end of the week.

AWE, BRING THE DAY

It's **9:00**am
Awe, you're so sweet
Awe, you couldn't know me better
Awe, thank you so much honey
Awe, you can always cheer me up when I'm sad
Awe, thanks for taking out the garbage
Awe, thanks for walking the dogs
Awe, I always knew you were too special
Awe, I hate that shirt on you because it makes me sick
It's **4:00**pm now
Awe, even the way you look in the fridge pisses me off
Awe, whenever you call, your ring tone is farts
Awe, the way you're able to act so comfortable with company
Awe, is your shoelace untied? Too fucking bad
Awe, thanks for the burnt toast (again) honey
Awe, yes dear, the aroma of cedar is wonderful
Awe, the way you make a list for everything is very freeing
Awe, how you make secret lunch dates at the diner
Awe, your breath smells like shit again
11:00pm, finally
Awe, I'm going to pray that you'll be gone in the morning
Awe, I am a fountain of crying agony because of you
Awe, I think I'll buy an Xbox tomorrow, or maybe a dog

DANCING SCHOLARSHIP?

Ok, I get it. You're not serious about the dancing. Ankle weights. The Humboldt Fog happens to be extra potent in this wheel. Meeting new people. Flowing on through. Getting all the gifts wrapped. Talking in circles. Not getting much done. Waiting on a phone call. Feeding parking meters is only for adults. Rated #**1** cancellation fee in the country. Wading through Rotten water and fishing for malleable creatures to turn into back scratching soldiers. Dry skin. Wet hair. Christmas morning.

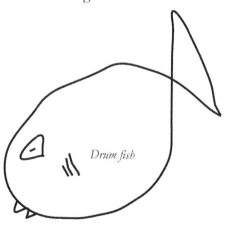

Drum fish

MONUMENTIAL MORALS

Ahhh the hunt! And for which it
stands, the unbeatable aggressor. High and
mighty. Fighting for human nature to be the
closure. When their bodies are armories.
Cages of remorse. When it's all wrapped up.
That winking eye. The haze of abandonment.
The returning tick that'll spoil the tock. Or
maybe even the long drive home. Those are
the keys that open the cages. This drowning
engagement that seems to be reoccurring, it's
not very interesting to me anymore. It's more
like Chinese torture. While my mind is running out of erasers trying to solve the equa-
tion my body is running into people on the
subway. I think these people are mad because
I ruined all their theories. I'm ruining even
the slightest appeals for hope. Because all this
monument is, is a false security and everyone
else is blind to it. When the bond has been
broke, the building will fall. It was built to
fail, just as a knife is made to stab.

Where I eat in the morning is the
same place where I write my rent checks.
Separating business from pleasure is hard to
do. Separating values from anything is the
first sign of danger.

THE MORNING RUN

     I want to see that wretched moment where you twist and then bow. As if anyone in your audience can't see the shadows. That place in your head where your vision gets clouded. When you're running in circles trying to find a balance. When you're rewriting your notions just to lure another lover. All that hard work and you're building castles out of playing cards.

     I'd like for you to feel that burn. You could find a forest and live there forever. You could find it like you found your mommy's bottle of piss and shit at the bottom of her laundry basket. Now I want to go prison painting. I want to design your interior. I'd put bells and whistles on your walls for all the tourists to gawk at. You'd be heating up some Spaghettios in the microwave before your shift at the hardware store. I'd be loading the shotguns and unfolding maps, highlighting trails.

     I believe there should be a coffee mug found on the next page. It is steaming with wet dew and fresh herbs, for your morning run of course. You'll be lacing up those brand new Fila's in no time. Such a boost of energy you'll have from the wonders that surround you. You understand that the things that grow effortlessly are really all that matters. Like cocks and pussies, I mean, they do grow effortlessly. There is no *training program* or black plastic battery capsule.

I remember when my teachers told me not to use too many "I's" in my work. I'm on a good one. What would they have to say about it now? I'll loose sleep just thinking about it, you know I have a sleeping problem. Yeah, I can't keep my eyes closed. Honestly, the only time I do close my eyes is when I'm turning the color of toilet water from crystal clear to dark brown.

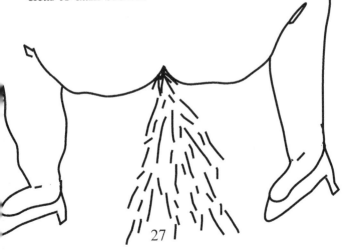

"SECRET SAUCE"

What a hungry bunch *wolves* just sitting there with their rifles and their bags of money. "Should'a bought a gun" I kept telling myself. I was instead preheating the oven for some wretched whore when I missed the revolution wagon. She was going to be *so happy* once she had her BBQ chicken pizza. Trying to cook chili in that empty house wasn't much easier. Stepping over trash bags of clothes everywhere was enough to notice a cycle. I pictured her carrying around these trash bags her whole entire life, like a blanket her parents brought her home in from the hospital.

KANSAS SPECTACULAR

I think we all know better than to just open up someone else's fridge and start opening shit, but *sometimes* it's ok. If someone had just gone to the store, then you could open up one item of your choice, that's the rule. I'd choose hawt dogs. Sally would choose a pepper. Jack would choose a cheese. Then we'd all scurry over to the fireplace and get super cozy. We would all melt our chosen items together and put them on some crackers or bread. It was almost like a widdle baby snack time, for a baby. We were all cuddled up close by the fire and father would make us stick our feet in the coals every so often. It was a learning experience. I am thankful. Daily bread = Full moon.

Shitty looking baguette

THE DARKEST DAY

If that day ever happens, I suppose it'll be quite the change. Persian shield. I'd like our natural food sources to thrive under large oak or maple. I would settle right above a youthful river, some bright white cabin with one big window. There have been a number of heated discussions concerning the installment of tire swings and zip ties. In my head I feel like I'm arguing with Danu.

There isn't much else to dwell on but your harvest. That is your only ticket, that and a heavily guarded perimeter. Personally, I've decked my halls with VS-**50**'s all the way up to the summit. Like fucking urinal cakes at the Staten Island landfill.

That old salmon rush won't hurt much either, until fluoride shows its face. A mineral with many branches, despite its array of potent toxins it has also brought hope. I don't believe the fish would benefit though. Let me introduce Mr. Efavirenz, a very powerful antiretroviral drug. Maybe it seems like cancer is the laser pointer and Mr. Efavirenz is the dog.

EQUAL BOUNDRIES

Between young **38** year old Bobby and the haunted mind of his elderly mother, there was nothing they couldn't do. Relying on each other day in and day out. What a beautiful *connection* they must have had. But now they have parted, Bobby went back to teaching ESL in Arizona and his mother went back to being man fondue in El Paso.

APPLE SCENTED CANDLES

My favorite self-inflicted false tradition happens to be a house that always smells like apple cinnamon candles. I suppose I just had a knack for them at an early age. I fell in love with the flickering. I was lighting tons of candles by age **10**. Now I practically live in a Yankee Candle factory.

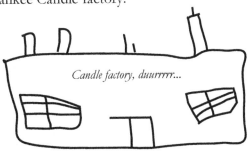

Candle factory, duurrrrr...

CARAMEL APPLE ANTELOPE

You take in account the **47** antelope deaths this year and multiply them by the amount of caramel wells and try to explain to me why you think people aren't eating them as snacks. The antelope are being dipped in caramel, brah. Don't think otherwise.

REASONABLE INCREASE

You see it in the news and now you're reading it on your mothers grocery list(s). When you try to pronounce it, your tongue gets real sticky. You are out of touch with today's top products, how do you feel you'll survive? Without a drivers license too? Your chances of "making it" another year are reasonably slim. *Reasonably* grim.

> *'Oh questionable being,*
> *thy precious bread, seeded today,*
> *and now in my oven,*
> *awaits your presence.*

-Breadboy

TRAVLEING WARRIOR

I've heard of this warrior who hangs eucalyptus on his bathroom walls and bags of rice on a door frame in his kitchen. Its been documented by thousands of historians that he was known to be soothed by these elements. The warrior would come home to a mess everyday. He would spend *all day* carrying rocks around in the desert. It was these elements that got him through the shivering nights.

Life wasn't so bad at The Asylum for this young warrior though, once a week his roommates would let him knead dough to make spaetzle. It would be this meal he would have to survive off of until his next kitchen privilege. His door was bolted shut at **10**pm and his alarm was loud and proud, promptly at **6**am.

Now he's married.

33

BARE SNOW CLAWZ

I accidentally parted way with the cap to my soda bottle. I had an earache and wasn't thinking brightly. Lately I've been reaching around and making things fit. Telling myself not to say too much. Not to spill the liquids and to keep quiet. I'm like a narrow stairwell with **1,000** keys on the ground. Maybe I'm not though, *you know?* Maybe I'm like a snow bear slapping fish out of the water with my finger fangs. RAWR!

Do you know what tastes better than cherries? Various types of artificially flavored cherry candy. Take it to the bank, cash it, *do whatever the fuck* you want with it. Every morning I dust a collection of feel good times, I drink ice cold sodas and shoot dart guns at the neighbors kids from my bedroom, 2nd floor. Mexico is **15** miles down the highway.

PRIME RIB

No sir, it's not Manwhich. This isn't going to be some quick *one-pan* meal for the staff. We're actually gonna grill up some real meat. We're going to throw it on my brothers **"BBQ pit"**. It's going to burn nicely, I'm sure some of my brothers neighbors will smell it and ask you for a bite. You can feed them from the deck like a mother feeding her babies. Chewing up the meat and hocking it over the threshold. You still get a *good amount* of flavor containing juices that way anyhow.

I want to let you know that my brother's neighbors will not, and cannot feed themselves. This isn't **2089**, food doesn't just grow on trees. My brother and me would greatly appreciate the kind favor of you feeding the neighbors. We've had too many run-ins with them and they won't take food from us anymore. They're practically withering away on their couches and lawn chairs. I've noticed a few that stare at TV's that aren't even turned on. They need to be fed before things get worse. Electric bills aren't being paid and everywhere I walk people are peeking out of their blinds at me. Apocalypse?

LEAPS AND BOUNDS

If there was ever to be a more complex indoor crawling facility, tell me, I'll pay your admission. I've seen kids stuck in ruts before, twirling their hair and humming super loud, not moving. It can be tempting to give up after being stuck in plastic catacombs for a couple hours. Beyond that, I'm just extensively curious about the baby changing stations I saw there. Are they safe to eat off of?

As seen on TV: *Turn your trunk into a baby changing station in a matter of milliseconds!* Or even design it as a permanent baby compartment while you're traveling long distances. They've been dipped bra, these babies have been dipped in their own brown messes and gently set on the doorsteps of America's most prestigious youths. Meow.

I've received tons of e-mails from rug companies the past few months. They're asking me to step all over their soft patches of cashmere stitched and cross stitched carpet selections. Can you imagine a patchy meadow of carpet from the den to the kitchen? It's like adult hopscotch for pussies. Hardwood, for life baby.

BANGKOK HOSPATALITY

I have a private fully functional **3**-bed hospital in my basement with **5** around the clock employees and **20** on call. I have one chef who is, *at heart*, a temper tantrum scientist who just happened to get his ass licked by nutrition one night. His current project is to manipulate living flesh to act as soil so you can harvest whatever you want that grows in the dirt, right on your own body. With the addition of micro root technology of course. Imagine, a fresh patch of tomatoes flourishing right behind your ear. I'd put a strawberry patch right between my wife's pussy and her asshole. Then I'd grow mint in her mouth so her breath wouldn't smell like a baby's shit caked diaper every morning. Barf.

Now it's my second day in Bangkok and I am seriously walking around like a retarded **10** year old. I say **10** year old because I have sense of flavor and would know how to dance if something happened. I just don't understand anything that's going on around me and I also can't read anything. I can't count money and most likely, if I just point to stuff I want on a jukebox, I'll probably be ordering something like liver or guts.

SMOKED SALMON

I noticed a salmon benedict right there on their menu. Being familiar with their more traditional benedict's, I was quick to order the salmon. The menu however, neglected to mention that the salmon was smoked, and I only like smoked salmon when it's cold, with cream cheese, and chives, maybe on a cracker if I'm lucky. They tried to make it look real fancy, piled high. I was more than unimpressed, this fish had just taken over the flavor of everything on the plate. Wishful thinking does in fact burn calories. The whole experience was like building your own tacos at a baby changing station, with shit smeared on the walls.

I'll just stick with the **19**th Hole from now on, maybe order some chicken fried steak or biscuits & gravy. Their BLT isn't half bad either, unless you don't like bacon, then it's probably more than half bad. I had fun stealing all the shows, I had fun *extending* my helping hand to single parent households. Nothing surpass' the amount of fun I had excavating my wife's asshole in the janitors washroom though. I feel sorry for her every time I go back in there. Gum dropz.

EDEN WONDER

Oxtail soup. Immune defense. Bugle Boy. Natural springs. Social media. Canyon mix. Moisturizer. Post-it's. Online banking. Porno. Boat shoes. Help me Rhonda. Medicine landfill. Punk rock. Circulatory system. Waking marvels. Widow's watch. Average reuben sandwich. California gold rush. Architectural configuration. Gluten free. High tech. Speed limit. Federal regulation. Food chain. Zero gravity training. Sourdough bread. Pristine objects. Dragon roll. Talent show. Intense pain. Bomb shelter. Palm springs. Retrospective exhibition. Ruff stuff. Siamese twins. Rising crust. Rotten world. White sox. Airport. Insomnia. Creative space. Time lapse. Bruised kidney. Ballet. Every age. Chicken hearts. Fragrance complex. Go green. Cluster fuck. Electric chair. Picture. Cultural differences. I am. Garden burger. Millville, Pennsylvania. Newly weds. Criminal intent. Boxcar derby. Wish list. Bumpy nipples. Hawt melk. Pot roast. Figment. Hike. Boston lager. Whirl wind. Dog training. Dead weight. Various memorabilia. Fine grain. Steak neckk. Power surge. Road trip. Stretch marks. Risky vision. Truth or dare. Debt relief. Family dinner. White walls. Beastiality. Cargo van. Windmill. Log cabin. Wonder woman. Sour cream. Ongoing investigation. Regional free. Iron will. Iron clad. Wet pussy. Ice cold American beer. Charred hot dogs. City zoning. School bus. Dance music. Electric box. Sideways. Red door. Avocado soup. **1,000** mile drive. Lightning. Ladder. Pain killers. Radio station. Radio boy. Front door. Single lane. Peak. Bed skirt. Frozen yogurt. Baby bottle. Checkers. Lots of drugs. Putting cigarettes out on carpet. Light rain. **No idea**. Regret. Power bottom. Cup cakes. Dictionary. Internet. Holler. Playboy status. Peppered steak salad. Waterfront. **6**am. Coke binge. Sunny side up. Rugrats. Graveyard. Nothings changed. All over again. Bobble wobble.

Cycle over.

JUSTIFIABLE SECRECY

The force in here is amazing because it's all so much different. No false sensitivities or reasonable doubt. It's just your insurance agent changing a few things around on your "love" contract. Post it where you want it, to serve and protect. Best pastrami sandwich in town right there. I've perfected absence like your mother's obnoxious manicure perfects the meaning of disparity.

Stepping into a cup of fruit – into a weak chicken broth – right into an unborn ocean – on someone else's precious property – on a light year century – into an establishment for some Phở – right smack dab on your roommates bath towel- on a pile of shit show compact disks – into the horse stables to feed and pet – on someone else's precious little beach front property – at the computer station working all the modules – on the gravel, roaming up that drive way in Pennsylvania – into the sidecar of Roman Rogers **1952** Vincent Comet – from the high dive and into the community pool – onto lovers lane – into a house of mirrors – onto an acre of sage and peppermint – on a pedestal and hidden far away.

SNORKLE ORACLE

I ended up swimming about **25** feet down to the bottom of an irresistible ocean bed. I wrote down everything in the sand with the fin of some elderly fish. This is what it said, they are the things I've done:

Third year. Manifested. Motive. Gotham City. Mexicali Cavern Tavern. Dairy. Trolley station. Cable car. Under dog. Bright smile. Land slug. Legal representation. Cedar bug out. Traditional sting operation. Beep beep. Potato cancer. Rodger Dodger. Cornmeal bugout. Open fairways. Chomping at the bit. Joint support. Fostered abandonment. Shin guards. Stole 20 bucks from mumsy. Whole pineapple. Brown bag. Satin sheets. I luff everystuff. Payton Womaning. Hallmark supper. Four card masterpiece. NuNu's kitchen menu. Soaking wet pussy. Took a seat. Toll booth. Smashed a castle. Whiplash syndrome. Put-put breakfast time. PBR tall can. Nozzel fizz notch. Carpeted shoe soles. Christmas lights. 1890's dream.

I surfaced a long rope of endearing pleasure, upward then outward. I assorted my motives with the future in mind. Hawtmelk.com

PLAYING FOR KEEPS

Tricks with mirrors; To instill fear and anguish into our daily lives and to feel the restlessness and regret that comes shining in through the blinds come dawn, *that* is the purpose of reflection. I twirl my hair in accordance with the longing I have to discover an occupational travesty among co-workers. To be able to control and manipulate people, just as my superiors have done to me. I like to keep the tradition going on, but only because I have nothing else to Jimmy crack corn. I'll crack corn till the sun comes up if I have to. I'm like a conservationist for eatable destruction.

The times I've spent on boats have been minimal, and I'm devastated because of it. Watching water come out of a tin-can tied to a sting is very close to a busy signal, of clarity. The motive that arises when observing skid marks on an airstrip is to connect the dots, to make letters - then words. I'm not exactly sure, maybe end up reading a book or something. The only time well spent for you, is when you're standing next to the microwave, waiting for your fucking T.V. dinner. Ding.

UPWARD ONWARD

I'm not waiting for someone to throw a frisbee out of a private jet you know? I'm just waiting for the commercials to stop, *stop*, it's my favorite show. What the mother fucking shit!?

Onward, upward, the way the crow flies. She's like a black cat scratching at the fixed angles of my ladder while I'm trying to paint the town of Bixby. Not really causing any harm, just making me overdose on superstition pills. I ended up buying over **50** red ties last week and I'm practically sewing them together to keep warm, because I spent all my money on them. That's the kind of shit that I'm talking about, the kinda shit that stains your mouth. Like the fucking trick gum that Pee-Wee Herman gives Francis in *Pee-Wee's Big Adventure*, and what a glorious moment that was.

One time I thought I was actually leaving for a different country, but it turned out that I was only being taken back to where I had been born. The old mill, right down there by Cranberry Muffin Street. Smelled good too. Salmon. Spawn.

ONE NIGHT IN KANSAS

If scratching is the devil then I can only assume rubbing is the hail marry, cause I'll take nearly **50**. Yeah, rub that cottonseed oil all over the bathroom tile and give it a chance to soak in. O my lord, the aroma will be just delightful, and then I'll say, "Hello all! Welcome to *my* world, my slumbers of eve, my palace of predispositions" and I'll say it proud. You'd walk through the hallways in search of food, and I'd leave bread crumbs in all of the west bedrooms for you. I would guide you through the harshest of times and make you live up to the promises you've made me and your bradders.

Ever want to build a dam? Ha, well it's too late fuckers, I already built one. I made it out of sticks and bubble gum(z). Yankees baseball Starter jacket. He didn't seem too happy with it, but none the less, I had a pizza delivered to my hotel with all the money I made. I tend to dream of enjoying the *simple things in life,* and making way for the rest you see. I like the idea of it but can never dig my beak into it. At least I can still take baths at the YMCA. Dig my beak around in there.

I HOPE THIS HURTS

I'm just kidding, I already know it won't hurt. It's not like I'm going to make you watch a season of Nickelodeons *All That*. Do not mention the motions I get when sleezing tomskins all around Miami in the olden day cars. Wishful thinking kind sir, wishful fucking thinking, and the typewriter goes *clip-clap*, *clip-clap*. What shouldn't do thy justice is the presence of mayonnaise at a neighborhood dinner function, keeping way. All about the neighbored tomskins they seem to be, but underneath their family room rugs are secret mail rooms. The functionality of tradition itself lie within the envelopes like Christmas checks from your insurance agent. I know somebody who is constantly over-cooking prime cut steaks like they're fucking pieces of toast. Every time I eat dinner at her house it's like playing Russian Roulette.

I feel like I should be cutting wood right now instead of writing this book. But this truly is my priority so I'm going to try and power through it. Most of the time I feel like swim-ming, and holding my breath, and being at the bottom looking up at the distorted view, it can be very kewl at times. Spurz.

CHRISTMAS PRESENTS

Who do your parents think they are to say what's a Christmas present and what isn't? Every *live-long* day my lunch is a fucking Christmas present to myself. However so gently, just because I treat myself with such self-pride and spill-proof angst doesn't mean I don't render tradition. I'm not like your brother sitting in the corner, feasting on my finger nails every couple weeks when they grow back from the previous buffet. Yes sir, I think that clears a few things up.

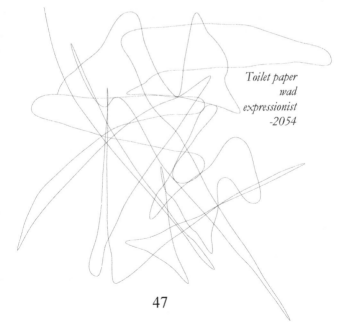

*Toilet paper
wad
expressionist
-2054*

ANOTHER LIKE YOU

The main reason that any other is just like it's *'nother* is due to friction in the bathrooms, it could be compared to a scrubber, scrub'n on that shit squatter, but it's really just two secretly familiar bodies. They're in conjunction to function and if you found the scripture I sent out to sea - you'd know more than well. My landlords husband John thinks it's complaining when you request for the jungle in the backyard to be trimmed, with a lawn mower, *a common activity in America I thought*. I've never met him, but rumor has it he teaches middle school, and if he ever gets lippy with me I'm gonna tell him that maybe if he was smarter they would let him teach older kids. Haha.

MOMMY TAKES SEDATIVES

I used to look forward to coming home and watching Wishbone on PBS after school, even in my early high school years. What a grand foundation the values taught in that show have built underneath me. Whenever I come to remember good times I've shared with inanimate objects I quickly stop myself, because it never happened. The only exception would be during my Tetris days, soon after I learned playing Pogs was fucking stupid.

There was a time in my life when I really enjoyed Stouffer's French bread pizza, when I was stupid - and peaceful. That was all the way back when I had to get rides from Don's chauffeur, shit was wonders, I was about 16. Pretty good age to start catching snakes and drowning them in water. Speaking of water, I went to the ocean yesterday. I wrote more crazy shit and thought about where I'd be if I was a mathematician, probably working for some chocolate factory in or around Columbus, Ohio or France.

HAVEN'T YOU EVER FELT

Guilty for something you did the morning after? Guilty for stealing a pinch of weed from your friends every time you see them. Guilty for eating tacos from Jack in The Box or a *double-chee* from MacDonnies. Lucid from eating too much chocolate while sun bathing, you're not a cat, so wake up. Livid from dealing with a neighbor because he plays his video games super fucking loud? Oh, and they're fucking recon strikeout video games too. Creeped out because you realized your property manager is the one who moved your clothes from the washer to the dryer? *Free of charge*. Oh, and he's a **70** year old weirdo that sells convenient parking during every baseball game, even if it's **100** miles away. Unlucky that you didn't get past security without them wanting to stick their fingers up your butt hole again? It happens every time you go on vacation. Beaten and battered when you roll around in the sun and bake in the sand - like a sandman appetizer? Scared to look back cause you think that guy you still owe **$200** is behind you? And he just got back from a UFC fight. Stupid for never trying anything other than ceaser salads wherever you go, cause you're a plain, dual, picky ass bitch? Forgetful for missing your last **3** doses of flaxseed oil? No wonder you can't move.

Every once in awhile I'll have a bagel for breakfast, one with cheddar cheese and jalapeños mixed in with cream cheese. It's usually on an everything bagel and it's pretty tard, and I bet only a few people can name where I get it from. I'll add I should just start making it myself. There's never enough jalapeños and they're never even spicy. *Buzz kill.*

jalapeño

MR. BIG NOISE

I knew this guy who insisted on com-
paring anything and everything to how it was
"kind of" like churning butter. Fucking any
girl can be like churning butter, I guess it just
matters how long it's been sitting out in the
sun for. I think the next terrorist attack
should be at Whole Foods, at the food bar, to
poison all the sheppard's. But hey, please
leave the soups alone.

I want to experience a shit load of
parades and carnivals in small towns this summer. They're pretty interesting and no one
knows how to speak Spanish except for the
line cooks at any diner. I bought everyone in
that place a pair of prescription glasses and
asked them what the fuck they were looking
at, like they've never seen anyone not finish a
plate of food before. Microwaved pizzas and
chocolate malt shakes. Reminds me of a time
when I had my whole life ahead of me. Back
when we use to hang out in the dirt hills.

RETURN TO SALVAGE BAY

Instead of sitting inside and watching television in your free-time you should go outside and sit in the grass somewhere and look around. I'm sitting in a park somewhere and I'm by a wooded hill. There isn't too much doubt that the two Mexicans I just saw weren't croaking on their dicks. I overheard them talking about lunch and I think they get sandwiches at the same place as me. Hawt coals.

Kids need two things: pizza boxes and public drinking fountains. Think about the message that sends to China, and all the basketball players out there. They also dink a lot of water. Someone I know probably woke up with a slice of pizza tattooed on them last week. I know it happens.

Public drinking fountains

Basketball

YOUR DADDY ISSUES

*Imagine you just got off work at **2:30**am and you drove straight to your work studio, there was some stupid rave deal at the adjacent "business".* Never mind - I'll just tell you first hand, because I can't deal. His mom fucked his dad with a broom handle, his dad had a dildo underneath his bed with shit on it. Some stray walked into my studio and someone's lover decided to converse with him. He said his dads dick was about as big as his and he would be forced to take a shit before his dad fucked him. He is wearing super puffy Adidas' and has a silver stud in his left ear, he's been asking for beer and cigarettes for the past hour. He has admitted to being on ecstasy and I'm about to ask him to leave. Because I'm tired and I'm not hungry for any leftovers. Writing is getting weird for me. He's **35** and he can't stop freeing Willy. The only thing that would top this shit is if he was writing a children's book, and I don't want to give him any ideas. His name is Terry, *fuck*.

Aside: *It's not about the size of the jelly-bean, it's about the size of the party.*

54

TALENT FRIENDLY

Its not fluffy like they wanted it, and why they wanted it fluffy I'm not sure. It's not a pillow, they're just lovely birds either way. I ate at a Cracker Barrel in Oklahoma City one evening during a very strong storm, I know I got mashers and gravy. I believe I was staying in a Marriott, they wouldn't let me swim in the pool or take a shower, it was like being on house arrest with an open door policy, kinda like Alcatraz. Everything just melts, like steak in your mouth. This chick I work with bent over to pick up a silver dollar and farted super loud, right in front of the prince of Egypt. It could have been a sand dollar though, I was by the living wall with not much of a view.

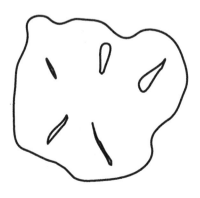

SCRAMMING TUFF

I've been talking with this agency who thinks they're the top posh-wobble-wobble-posh-ganache of everything known to showbiz. In the night I stay awake in my red sheets and talk to my brother, about whether or not I should get the surgery. Flat bottom girls make me sick, and girls with cheap shoes make me sicker, and girls who wear dirty white flip flops, what about them!?. Any girl with manicured finger nails or toes between the ages of **18** and **30** will probably fuck you, think about it. It really isn't as much of a talent show as you think, it's kinda like spaghetti – it always tastes the same.

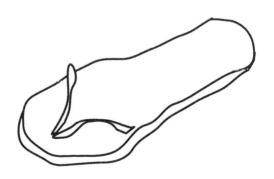

MANAGING FLAVOR

Is managing seeded bread, is managing two different reels, is managing drug addictions, is managing gas mileage, is managing overdraft fees, is managing day old bread, is managing a life crisis, is managing not caring about political welfare, is managing not to pay attention to the homeless, is managing thinking about sautéing cockroaches in a chimmichurri sauce, is managing not to think twice.

CARPET CITY FAIRGROUNDS

My family bought those expensive paper towels today, the really absorbent ones. I've been using the same piece as toilet paper for the past week. This is Carpet City, the place where everyone gets super cozy. There are children here who cannot go a day without a slice of pizza from Lugis, they are *Rotten World*. They are cottonseed oil, mixed in with the French fries for a fancy finish. They are the people at A, B, C & D towing. They are people pretending to be of the opposite sex with fake names.

PUPPY CHOWDER

There is an opera this weekend at the fair grounds and I'm inviting the whole city. I'm gonna invite Olympians and dragons and cooks and movie producers. All we're gonna do is roll around in carpet and mix punches together. Somewhere out in the land of America once lay Ye Olde Wyandot Lake, a water park for suburban middle class hermits. People who would be happy to represent your client, or lend a hand grilling steaks at your baby's Easter party. They are the management, and their cruel intentions are masked by persuasive offers and magazine subscriptions. To open up a false bank account all they would need is a receipt from a grocery store proving they bought over $20 worth of vegetables grown in Mexico. Free checking, CD's, Bond's, you name it. All on paper, recycled paper, go paperless now. Pepper, not paper.

No thank you, I will not have the paper.

PANTY LINER

The uniform he hides behind, and the scam that packs his britches, young Carlos at the tow-yard, with his(?) thinking cap on. With her flat top buzz cut. I've traveled through territory where warehouse flem bound their offspring, where they manufacture coal and try to get diamonds and shit. Not anything like SLC thought, their salt communities over there are secret and in order. I just bought The Book of Mormon the other day for a dollar, I don't know if I'll read it or not but I will take it with me next time I venture to SLC, maybe some local will buy me lunch there or something. BYOB.

HOUSING A BEET GARDEN

Local, organic, sustainable products. That's what it's all about. I have this friend who stands under this blinking light, he thinks of ideas and jots them down in Christmas cards. Three years ago he bought a lot of stock Christmas cards on Ebay. Some seasons never change. I stare at my glass of wine with the faint sounds of a movie in the background, I think about the flames and their patterns of aggression. There is proof in the air, but the wires always tend onward, tied like the shoes of a cub scout. *There was a fire today*, approaching midnight there was a fire.

I walked around the pool and got to see what people were up to. I cleaned up their plates and glasses, I cleaned up after them, pretty much wiped their asses. I washed all their dirty dishes in the hot tubs and drank their half full champagne bottles on a made up trip to dry storage. Some of the girls at my work, they snap like fingers, it's funny. That's funny, *this* is funny. They snap like fingers, they walk on tight ropes, they complain about people ordering their sauce on the side, and they don't like repeating things. I keep feeling things crawling on me.

BOTTOMS UP, BULLDOG

He hates that Miss Farmer, she's such a fucking bitch. Last night I walked up to golden hill to get some red wine, it got really interesting pretty quick. I passed by someone on the other side of the street who I've stuck my dick into before. A girl. A guilty pleasure, a longed for lover, a carrot on a string. The bulldog who guards these gates is easily distracted by a half pound of peppered turkey breast (just like your fat ass dad) and some steel toed boots, on sale. If you read them lullabies they'll certainly dream civil. Civil is as civil does, but what civil needs, never was. Civil's face, gone flushed with fear and his trembling hands, reaching for the gears. The machine shuts down and everyone's off, what a hard day at work, what a night so soft. Tomorrow the gardener comes at **8**, last time he stepped on all my peppers and emptied out all my pots onto the side walk, like a wizard, looking for *cans* to collect. I collect cards, wizard cards and Magic decks in any condition. Just kidding, never that.

FOLDED

I once met a leaf eater, he ate the seed out of my palm but that doesn't make him a seed eater. Survivor. The man in the mirror. The man who puts a little bit of dill in everything. Who is he? Not Jesus, nope. Just another citizen whose decided to bring an un-likely herb into a whole new world.

Lots of white space under here.

O YA, IT'S REAL DARK

The prisoner isn't caged. Any product is a prison, any nurture is a poison. We are prisoners to gravity, we are prisoners to envy. I caught this turtle in Pennsylvania one time, it was black, light green, dark orange and brown. I left it in a milk crate and when I came back an hour later it was gone. I put a shit ton of leaves in there but I guess that wasn't enough, *I mean*, you should have seen where he was living before, in a stink'n pile of sticks.

I remember rolling around in bed, waiting to walk to school in the morning. In Sophomore year I walked to school with this one kid, lets call him Pauly. He would wait on my door step with his coffee and hash browns from Burger King, he would mess with his red curly hair and smoke Marlboro Lights. He started wearing Abercrombie & Fitch and we didn't really talk anymore. He lives in Texas now with his beaty little polarized sun glasses. Living time is too short to get caught up in something like that, to corner yourself into a career at an early age is probably the worst, sticking your dick in the daily grind, selling yourself a loop.

METHOD START TRAM

All the darkness in just one room. There is a baby in the corner brushing the hair of an elderly dog, I can't tell what kind, maybe some sort of Lab/mix. Anyways, it's creepy, the whole thing, all of it, creepy. Creepier than me getting drunk off wine in my apartment by myself and watching things crawl on the walls. Creepier than your landlord taking it upon himself to move your clothes from the washer to the dryer and a week later you moving his clothes from the washer to the dryer and noticing he has a pair of your underwear. Yep. All this darkness, in just one room. They're asking me to leave. I'm more than happy to do so, her body language spells everything out, all over the walls like someone spilled coffee. The lights are flickering, the fridge sounds like an ant farm and I'm on my way out the door. Maybe I'll partner up with Christian in commercial real estate, he'll eat whatever type of pasta you give him, forget about everything else for that time being.

My agent told me that every time I chew with my mouth open I'll live another **40** years, he no longer represents me.

BROWN VITAMINS

Little tiny pills, little tiny landfills, little tiny astronauts. Always with the Rembrandtz, freezing their honey to savor the sweetness. Speaking of which, I'm squeezing one out right now, I'm letting the bags drop. Inside the bags are green sauce, hearts of palm, arugula and goose filling. They are combustible, but they're not hazardous, unless you don't like having a good time. Duck-du-uuuck-GOOSE! Keep running. Just like you keep running out of time, you filthy animal.

I'm taking my brown vitamins and loving every second of it, but lately there has been some heavy questioning going on. Is it weird that when I sit at my desk I'm starring at a picture of a door knob? Is it weird that I bought a black candle for the first time? I think so. Does it interest people when they ask me where I live and I tell them "skid row"? I think so. Is it common placement when I set two rocking chairs next to a bean bag? Does my neighbor really like video games that much?

MAMA BEAR
▮▮▮▮▮▮▮▮▮▮▮▮▮▮▮▮▮

I'm not sure how I ultimately feel
about it but the other day I was thinking that
it wouldn't be so bad to call a girl mama bear.
Like "wuzzup mama bear, WHERE YOU
AT!?". Not too bad right? *Anywaysie*, it might
not work on some stupid girl, or whatever,
but if you had porridge with you; I think you
could pretty much score anywhere. At least
anywhere I'd be caught dead. At least anywhere Pee-Wee Hurman would be caught eating bread.

There happens to be another mama
bear in town though. She hangs out one
block north of my apartment next to the Sal-
vation Army. Shes out there with her fucking
kid and nearly 10 other degenerates (who
brought their own chairs…to the corner!) just
ranting and screaming about nothing every
day. I think they sleep around there too, I've
been watching them through my window with
these binoculars that used to be my great
uncles. It's like watching the river flow, right
into the sewer system. Where crime fighting
turtles eat pizza and play checkers.

66

GLOBAL SHAWARMA

I have to say, it's been a treat thus far. I did this painting titled "Apple Stand Girls" and there is an airplane in it dropping bags of shawarma. The bags look like potato sacks tied tight with rope. I think the people of this nation should be happy. They want to eat the planet. Black houses, white windows.

We touched on the subject, we touched in real life. We ate apple pie and we made it our life. I wanted to keep all the slices for myself and hide them in a basement, change the locks and split town. But somebody already made their move, a familiar face. A bloody townsmen, a wretched soul!

I had this roommate one time for about a month or so, he was a cheese head, meaning, he ate fucking cheese all the time. I was wondering how he hadn't already melted in the sun…but I soon realized that it was because he never saw the sun. When he wasn't working as a bellmen in La Jolla, California he was sitting on my couch watching CSI and eating something with a shit ton of cheese on it. If there is anyone out there in the world, please talk to me about this.

GNOCCHI AS A SIDE PLATE

Aim for the gun and reach for the lettuce. Some think it's crazy but some think it's fetish. I just took the time to write **4** letters to some old friends, it's instant gratification. Like riding a motorcycle and thinking you're kewl. I also wrote a letter to an old landlord that still owes me $**700**. So much for daydreaming this one away. I've decided to award myself with one day in a chocolate factory, to make sure everything is running smooth, everyone should be doing their job.

I thought there'd be gnocchi, but we ended up just ordering some shitty pizza from some shitty waitress. Some shitty pizza I felt guilty for eating afterwards. I mean, I didn't just take a ferry across the bay for some freaker fucking pizza. It wasn't half bad though, it just made it's consumers avenge into the night without any regard to human decency. We ate raw meat and slept in bushes, we put orange construction cones on the roofs of cars, we dreamt of steak and slept on the finest of hardwood floors.

TANG WANG # 4

There was elderly man who got tied
up and pushed down the street. There was
tons of o's and u's, not like IOU's though, no
I's, kind of like yogurt. As in, he'd won the
lottery and spent it all on some Indonesian
family to build and sponsor gardens that feed
the village. Which is precious, but I'm pretty
sure they've been feeding themselves for cen-
turies now. Now he has to wheel himself to
the Alberson's to buy kitty litter, for his kitty.
I wonder if he feels weird passing by veget-
ables that cost six dollars a pound.

Tang Wang is an honorable mention.
Her nose is practically falling off, which is
practical, if you want your nose to fall off.
She mulls around the streets with her Ern-
heart derelict looking for cans and leaning up
against buildings that read "free job training"
on their signs. Her nose seriously looks like
blacktop with dead white skin on the ground.
Almost like frostbite or a charred steak. But it
turns out they've just been dipped in caramel,
brah. I have one hour left, one hour to see
the things I've always wanted, to see the
things I've always thought of, one more hour
till Bread Crumb City.

FAITH & LOVE

Each July I make faith jelly. I portion out the preserves into mason jars (yes, like grandma) and drill them shut, right into a cabinet, where they'll await for a fall harvest. A full moon, an old man with a huge white band-aid on his feverish head stumbles by an east window. He has faith in only mirrors, because mirrors tell no lies. Love is a symptom that grows on your shoulders; your head pops off, and then you die, alone. So he has no faith in love, only faith in mirrors. What a fine candidate he'd make for the races this Tuesday. I had red ribbons and green tea cooling on my windowsill. I had lots of ideas last night, it was a breath of fresh air. There was a fever in the heart of the city, we were playing with traffic like we were playing with Matchbox cars. She made me nervous, but in a good way, she was a reality check. Gravy train, what a stupid thing. I'm not sure what else to say, I like egg sandwiches with mayonnaise and a little bit of butter, salt, and nothing but fluffy white bread. Reverb. To repent. Rod Stewart, if you think I'm sexy. There is something about her that screams fluffy white bread, and it's her ass. I gave her a riddle and she gave one back.

GUILT OF AN ENDLESS JOINT

That guilt of an endless joint, where
you can separate nothing but the best. The
flexibility. The finest in the business of
course, you can separate the time it took from
the feelings it dealt. I used to make prank
phone calls from my friends basement when I
was a sophomore in high school. We would
use a phone tap on one phone and play it
through the speakers. Recorded on a compact disk, but they all start out the same way:
"Hi, I was just in there about **30** minutes
ago…".

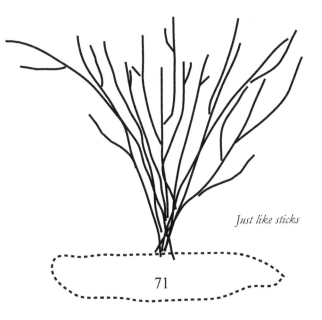

Just like sticks

71

NATIONAL ENSUREITY

I know a Captain Bollock, and he flies kites, ones of substantial size. He is known throughout his neighborhood as a hero, he is known throughout his community as a sure fit…until recently, old man Bollock got carried out of his day job by two security guards yesterday morning. He got caught opening up co-workers mail in the shitter stalls. After several employees had complained about not receiving pieces of mail the last few weeks, everyone has been on the hunt, 'ta put 'er 'ta bed. So Bollock got tucked in for mail fraud. In the stalls though, it seemed like he was on the other end of a glory hole. Yep, no one really knows, but he could have been working two jobs.

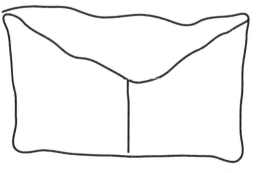

Envelope

LAS VEGAS

I know this guy that keeps a blanket in his trunk in case he gets into a fight with his girlfriend. I specifically asked him if that was the reason when I saw it, as he was loading bags of lard and assorted crackers into his trunk, in the parking lot of a Smart & Final. Someone's battery was getting drained at the time, it was mine.

This is Earf

MAID OF HONOR

The sister of Marie or something I think it was. Awhile ago she told me in a dream that I would shortly be meeting someone that would strike me as Pancake Boy. Well, last night I got struck. I got dipped, brah. Pancake Boy lives in a halfway house with some fat bitch who wears multiple little satchels around her lard-tard arms and smokes abandoned cigarettes she finds in the cracks of sidewalks.

None of it matters. I walked down the streets this evening and everything was empty. I mean, there was nothing, not even a hose left on or anything. All the traffic lights change right after another, it's like watching dominoes from some kids hard drive. Me and Shelly, linking up the rockers.

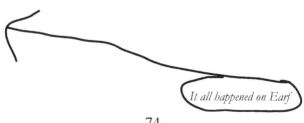

It all happened on Earf

REARVIEW MOMENT

The huckleberry stew we made is collapsing into a capsule and being taken all at once. How does that make me feel? It makes me feel like a teabag in a trashcan at some insurance office. Stuck. Stuck without the stew we made, stuck without the glue we saved. I'm tired of living life through these streets, I shouldn't be sleeping in the bushes with a record contract, not tonight, not tomorrow night. My rearview has yet to be deceiving but I only look when I'm leaving. Don't look back. Never that. Drew pimp. Turkey jerky.

HOTEL DONKEY

As I approached the rather tasteful Hotel Donkey late this morning, I noticed a gathering of strange buildings on the property, set back in the woods. The buildings were smaller in size and had tin roofs. They had very few windows and no places to park. I don't really care about the buildings, I just thought I'd share that with you. The next time someone tries to give me **3** magic beans as a tip I'm gonna plant them in the San Diego Zoo so all the animals can escape. The last beans I had I used on the golf course at Area-**51**. The results were freaker fucking good and patrons always had a blast during those days. Someone mentioned something about The Hotel Struz as well, but I didn't pay any mind to it.

Holiday Inn

DONNIE WHITE

His name is Donnie White, it's not
Donnie Reckless. There isn't a corner in
town even close to here where you could be
more reckless. Twirling. Thinking. Over
hearing this man who has names for all the
rings on his fingers. I heard a story passed
down through some friends about this one
guy named Jerry. Apparently Jerry passed a
homeless man on the side walk who appeared
to be exchanging words with some sort of
representatives. I thought that was funny.
My house is full of fridges and my fridges are
full of eggs, eggs in the kitchen. Like eggs in a
basket.

77

ALL TRIMMED UP

Just like a seaberry, swimming around in the unknown. Green waters make you sick while green river rapids make you squeezle. I found a broken key on the sidewalk and scrapped it up against a brick wall all the way home. It was kind of like watching someone named Mike scrape his teeth across a cob of sweet corn. Kind of like that, nothing goes to waste. What if the star athlete at your high school broke his foot trying to touch a load of sprockets from one of the windows in the grain room? Would you call in the forces to come retain the lad? Maybe not.

HEAT

TEMPER PEE DICK

Its kind of like sleeping on a slice of fresh ass fluffy white bread, homie. Meow. Aye, yo, you got that new Madden, homie, meow? Don't worry, they're just my cats. Talk a lot, eat a lot, sleep a lot. That's not a foreign tale, nor a far off one either. I feel like working at the Zoo and riding some tiger's coat tails into captivity so I can eat all their stews. Simba's kitchen. It's not the biggest kitchen in the world but it certainly isn't the smallest. No way - no how. Young Simba in all his glory, standing over the heat of the stove and looking like a French maid dusting garlic powder on some chicken breasts. Beauty is the beast. The beast is longing for a caption, something of relevance, some sort of message in the sky. While you were watering your plants and helping things grow your neighbors were fighting over nothing and breaking each other down. Maybe they should open the blinds some time and get some sun in there.

KICKERS TICKETS

They might even need some kickers, you know, those kickers tickets. The ones with the foiled tips, fancy tickets for a fancy time. At the kickers, at the top of the world. Your boss walks in on a huge paper football tournament in one of the conference rooms and you're leading the bracket. Promotion? I think so. See what happens at kickers this summer.

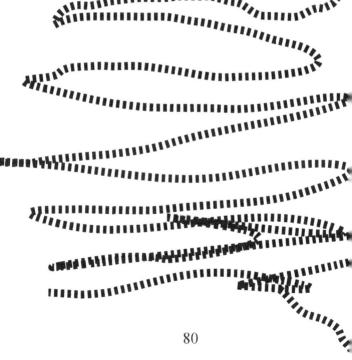

STATIC LOTION

Sanderz and blenderz. They all want to get in the sunrise, and forget about those fragments you hinder, what would you do with the information? Buy a salad, get into the sunrise? Ever feel like you woke up in the morning and rubbed static lotion all over your body? Try sleeping in dryer sheets, if that doesn't work, get on the internet, and if the internet doesn't work, try blowing lightly across the top of your keyboard.

The young soul with his delicate hands, carefully removes the reheated macaroni & cheese from the microwave and places it on the coffee table. He turns on the TV and unbuttons the top button of his shit. He blows on the macaroni & cheese like he would blow on a small fire. Without reason. To put out the fire is to savor the flavors as to put'n bay is toooo....tango the wafers. The vanilla ones, with their buttery crusts and perfectly moist inner texture, for the millions, the masses can eat wafers too! But only if they want. You see, it seems as if society has forgotten about wafers all together, right out the window, just like your great grandmother did with her bedpan. Out the window.

81

BEDTIME FLOWCHART

Cracker pot pie. Waiting game. Cooling down. Cash crop. Insurance waiver. High dive. Hotel guest services. Not understanding. Banana hammock. Goldie locks. Onion head. Up up down right. Being impressed. Times change. Babies sell drugs. Violin. Rat cave. Explanation. Painting like Pollock. Maximum comfort. Mummies in caves. Chicken tenders. Fender benders. Strange power. Time travel & robots. All my love. Building blocks.

Bedtime flow chart is not to be taken to any other levels, you must also have a cracker pot pie.

ONLY ONCE

I found someone sleeping in my jacket. I told them to get out, and "*SCRAM!*" I stole a cat off of someone's front porch and raised it as my own for a few months, it then got pregnant and gave birth to 4 kittens right in front of me. One was off-white with grayish finishing's, one was all gray and plump, one was various colors of orange and stripped, and the last one looked just like the mother, all the cats combined, it was the runt. The name of the mother was fucker, given by me in a cruel world. In a moment of absence I'd sprinkle water for them.

I know this cycle, *blah blah toos wamma*, it sleeps in the comfort zone of race car bed, and it looks out it's window only to see other windows. When it opens the window it opens the building blocks of a moderate concern. It scratches its fabric walls and steeps peppermint tea bags for all its top floor neighbors. Spreading the love, pressing the peddles. Its fabric walls don't muffle the sounds of the outside world, some fucking berry picker, some fucking…wild rice man and his raggedy old bible, walking down my streets with a megaphone talking all his new found bullshit.

SIDEWALK SLEEPER

Amongst the many of sidewalk sleepers I've seen pass through my **2**nd and **3**rd bases, one in particular stands out. This young man, probably in his early twenties, he ties whatever extra garments he has tightly around his waist if it gets too hot. Anyways, I was wondering why the fuck he was out here, with his suitcase and his clothes folded neatly inside. Why the shit storm was he out here, with his pocket watch and his cellular telephone. Looking at constellations like a child looks at a connect the dots book. Ya, I didn't get it, but then tonight I saw him being jittery, *like he had the god damn jitterz or somethin'!* Since that's out of the way now, we're gonna call him Turkey Boy, like it's Thanksgiving. Turkey Boy also appears to have an oven for the gentlemen, he gawks at every spike that *jams* by. He might be sitting on a magic carpet, I'm not sure. Is it weird to hand in a resume with BBQ sauce on it? Not if you're applying for a position at Applebee's. He went to the store to window shop for ankle bracelets, he wears the girls slip on Vans in black and white checkers. On occasion he enjoys reading a book, unfortunately, he won't be reading this one, now that he's in it, as Turkey Boy.

CRACKED PEPPER?

Both of these men changed their outfits before dinner. They meet these two common lassies and run around in circles over them. Sunday school was out and Winston Princeton Jr. & his curious father Mr. Winston Princeton finally had enough crumpled-up sweaty dollars to buy these lassies some culktails. My jar of peppercorns fell in the sink yesterday and now I can't crack pepper, I can't crack corn, and now I can't crack pepper. White socks and black socks. Winston Jr. once noted taking baths in olive oil and having your loved ones crack fresh pepper and Dominican sea salt all over you is like winning the lottery, and turning everything into shit that's lush. Olive oil baths are fucking lush, meow. I mean, what a treat, now you're a fundamentalist swimming (drowning) in your choice of any aromatic oil spill. You love the publication. You love Spaghetti pot.

We found loads of cream in the ground and we started buying out all the land and constructing plans for one of the worlds larges creameries. We wanted to make some cream and have some fun with it. Like a foam party in Spain.

85

ANGLE DUST TUCKER

Please don't give these angels any supper, they've been getting quite big the past few months and you sir, are the one who's been feeding them. So I must regulate your feeding procedure from here on out, you'll need supervision and much criticism. Where is her mail at!? *Who isn't innocent.* The food is burning, never mind it turned out good. I decided to sit here and take swigs of Jim Bean, to kind of get the blood flowing. However, as this may be one of few mentions, there has been many more occurrences. Not to abuse the privilege, no sir, but I'm not shy to its assistance. Let me also add, how many days have been ruined!? Take a stink'n look around ya'll. The mess we've put ourselves through and the neglect we have to ignore the issue is very **1870**'s. We can teach them English during their last minutes.

Jim **BEAN!**

BARBERSHOP

When I'm working at the barbershop
I feel like I'm cooking for the devil, all those
creams and knifes make me hungry too. I
never got hungry in a basement like the devil
thought. I found a rack of petticoats while I
was down there. If I was down somewhere
else I might have found a couple beef cur-
tains, if you catch my drift (wood). All this
shit is super kewl, shit I'd be the beneficiary
of, like sticks and stones. Ice cakes are fucking with my shit right now, but it's perfect this
way. Like a super cold reservoir and my teefz
are hyperventilating, *quick! Someone throw me a
lifesaver!* Today I was in this little lunch spot
and someone asked me what I thought this
guy across the way was listing to, *ha*, the
middle-aged overweight black guy with the
Kangol hat and the huge headphones…acid
jazz. *Duh.* Just like my uncles brother-in-
law's sisters fire-cracking fuck neighbors did
with Jungle **2** Jungle starring Tim Allan. Well,
now I'm just fucking with you, my uncle
doesn't even have a bradder. Well, it's my
birthday again, last time I had a birthday I
fucked my friends ex-wife at an embassy
suites in Detroit. I thought I saw Emenem
from my hotel window, pretty sure.

SCIENCE OF BUTTER

Please, take a piece of me with you. I feel like there's another fire and I want you. I need to put some on there. I want to build something, some sort of breakfast sammy. Kinda wanted it melted, kind of want it in a box to-go, MEOW, cause you're upsetting my family. Ya, no, I want to teach you.

I go check out a med school in New England that shall remain nameless, and to my surprise, the condition of the facility was almost torturous, students being chained to their beds and desks, reading and writing. Most of the kids ate yogurt that came in squeezable tubes, *you know the brand.* I have a really small dresser and some of these kids I just don't like. Some of the kids here where I live and some of the kids there, where they med.

MEOW, HOMIE

I have to tell ya though, you'd love
New England homie, meow. Hold on while I
scratch my neck and lick my belly. Hold on
while I make this telephone call, and look out
my northeast window. I saw somebody bite
someone by the tracks, it was almost like
watching the discovery channel and then flip-
ping to some story on the news about how
werewolves *are real people too.* I've seen them
in the movies and on candy wrappers, that's it
though.

Candy

MOTHERS WHEY

I took a piece of bread, I took a piece of butter, I spread it on the bread and I put the two together. I know a Mexican girl who was afraid to show me her vagina, her brown tinted drawbridge. Like the only reason she was horny was because she just got off her period. Or, I've come to find that most girls get horny if you just whip out a big dick. Sometimes I whip out a prosthetic dick just to get the mood started. Just kidding, I have junk. But I also have a shallow mind, it takes a very confused girl to weigh out which one is more amusing. They usually go with my dick, then we fight, and then I write. Then we break up, she looks for another dick, that seems caring (at first). I make money, and then spend it all on some bitch that just ran some other guys bank account slim and jim. It's kind of like hit or miss, but then again, beating around the bush is always a miss, anyone, triple balance beam, anyone, *Buller*?

Hawt azz melk homie, meow.

WAIT FOR IT

Waiting for this free internet to do it's job is like waiting for your microwave to cook some shitty ass dinner, while you're on speed. I heard the only reason everyone goes vegetarian is because your body goes through so many changes and you just get super fucked up. Like, this one Potato-head guy watched all 3 seasons of Lost in 24 hours. Only ate carrots.

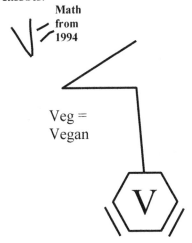

Math from 1994

Veg = Vegan

Somehow you're always right, just, so spot on!

BESIDES THE POINT

I wanted **3** packets of sugar, not **2**. I wanted to sweeten things up, but then I started to think about sweetener, and how it was more like fertilizer for lesser valued brain cells. I don't even like coffee either. I like booze, weed, pussy, and loud music. O, and sleep, sun, water, hotdogs, silk anything, *fuck*, what else, what do I (actually) like? Hmmm, I use other birds beaks to taste the dirt, if they want to get their beaks wet so fucking bad then why the fuck not. I might get my beak wet in some macaroni & cheese, you never know, we already know there's butter. There's street sweeping on these streets by my house...I never knew the city would pay some guy to stand on the sidewalk and spray a hose at some fucking dirt and chewed up gum on the ground. Or, I never knew society would walk or drive by people sleeping on the ground and get confused about whether or not they're capable of being productive. Like cleaning up gum and dirt off the ground. No middle man there.

I remember the Hotel Donkey.

TWENTY TWENTY

Some foreign wanker waltz' out of some tunnel grouping over by the harbor and at the top of his lungs screams "LETS GET SUPER COZY THIS YEAR!!!". To my surprise, he was right, he knew that no human being would ever be opposed to getting cozy, anywhere. The bloody wanker was spot-on. Something he must have learned in the tunnels. It wasn't a *spewage* system, it was a value system.

This morning was a nightmare, first someone burnt my toast and then I got stuck in traffic. What have I ever done to deserve that kind of treatment? Hi, I'm Donny Reckless. I find calling this town "Baby City" to be appropriate because that's the level of shit people complain about. There are **3** complaints; traffic, parking, and rain, oh, and someone wanting to fuck your midnight squeeze. Freshly squeezed, homie, meow. *Two things that are stupid, go, now:* Umm, break dancing annnnd…beat boxing. It's the only two things you can do with a piece of cardboard and a good amount of spit. Hwak-tuie.

35psi.

WEST VIRGINIA

Aunt Marry, Bob, Jim, Hippo, Faith, Silvia, Terracotta, and that devilish old hag Papa Bear. Do you think he'll mind if I call him Papa Bear? Anyways, that was the line-up for young Tom Favors visit to West Virginia, the *motherland*. He would roll in with his roll dog Danny, they'd roll into town on a dirt road. First heading in East on the **79** and then splitting south on the **33**, fucking chugging coffees the whole way. Danny cleaned some of the rifles on the way in, good boy, shoes tied tight. Always snacking. Lip smacking. They ran into some black guy with hair that looked like sticks, he said he had tricks and that he did his first stint of rehab in Kentucky. Then he had the heart to ask if someone was from Argentina.

Cotton mouth fudge factory. Turtle-dove-chocolate-treat. They sat around a campfire and played beauty parlor. They sat around a poker table and played barber parlor. They sat in their wardrobes and played ice cream parlor. They sat pretty much anywhere and did what they wanted to.

Well this is it, you've reached the end and
I know what you're thinking...

But please:
Be rational with your thoughts about life
from here on out.

Thanks.

Complementary grocery list!

- ☑ Beans
- ☑ Soup
- ☑ Tea
- ☑ Happy
- ☑ Water
- ☑ Bagel
- ☑ Ham
- ☑ Juice
- ☑ Cookies

Made in the USA
Las Vegas, NV
28 February 2022